D0532500

Work well from home

How to run a successful home office

BLOOMSBURY

A BLOOMSBURY REFERENCE BOOK

Created from the Bloomsbury Business Database

www.ultimatebusinessresource.com

© Bloomsbury Publishing Plc 2005

First published 2005 by
Bloomsbury Publishing Plc
38 Soho Square
London W1D 3HB

British Library Cataloguing in Publication Data
A CIP record for this book is available from the British Library.

ISBN 0–7475–7737–4

Design by Fiona Pike, Pike Design, Winchester
Typeset by RefineCatch Limited, Bungay, Suffolk
Printed in Italy by Legoprint

All papers used by Bloomsbury Publishing are natural, recyclable
products made from wood grown in well-managed forests. The
manufacturing processes conform to the environmental regulations
of the country of origin.

Contents

Could *you* work well from home?

Working from home is an attractive option for many people, but there is a lot to think about before you rush off to equip your office. Answer the following questions and then read on for advice on whether it's a good solution for *you*.

How often do you stay late at work?
a) Regularly.
b) Only if I have to meet a deadline.
c) Never.

Do you enjoy working as part of a team?
a) No; I don't like to rely on anyone else.
b) Yes, but I also enjoy working independently.
c) Yes. It means I can off-load tasks onto others.

How do you plan your daily tasks?
a) I write out a schedule and stick to it.
b) I make a list of the most important tasks and hope to remember the others.
c) I tackle jobs as they come up.

What do you do when faced with many projects at once?
a) I get on with the most important ones first.

b) I choose the most interesting job and start on that.
c) I start several tasks and continue with the easiest one.

How organised is your work space?
a) Very. I know where everything is.
b) Fairly. I have been known to lose things.
c) Not at all. I don't think about the state of my desk.

How do you feel about your boss?
a) I feel that he or she interferes at times.
b) We have a good working relationship.
c) I rely on his or her guidance.

How would you describe your relationship with your colleagues?
a) Lukewarm. I keep myself to myself.
b) Good. It's professional and friendly.
c) Great. I love the camaraderie of the office.

How do you react to unexpected difficulties?
a) I'm methodical and try to deal with the problem from its source outwards.
b) I try to follow solutions to similar problems in the past.
c) I'm not a great problem-solver and so I panic.

How would you describe the process of delegation?
a) I see it as laziness. If a job comes your way, it's up to you to deal with it.
b) It's an important process for the development of yourself and your staff.
c) It's a useful tool—if you haven't got time to do something, pass it on!

a = 1, b = 2, and c = 3.

Now add up your scores.

Everyone should read chapter **1** first as it's full of essential questions to ask yourself about how you might adapt to a home office.

- **9–14:** In many ways, you are ideally suited to working from home. You like to work independently and have no difficulty motivating yourself. In fact, the only problem might be that you would never switch off— you must think carefully about scheduling time for yourself. Chapter **3** will help you put some parameters around your working time. You may also have a tendency to isolate yourself from others. When you work at home, it's important to keep in touch with key colleagues and contacts; turn to chapter **5** for advice on this topic.
- **15–22:** You appear to have a balanced attitude to your working life and should adjust well to working from home. Don't underestimate, however, the upheaval of adjusting to a new routine; you should lay down careful foundation plans. Chapters **2** and **3** should stand you in good stead. Also, you may need some help prioritising your tasks when you're on your own. Turn to chapter **4** for advice on how to work out what needs doing and when.
- **23–27:** You thrive on working with others and should think very carefully about whether you would make a smooth transition to working from home. You will have to work hard to motivate yourself and you may

feel isolated. Chapters **3** and **5** will help you make the adjustment, while chapter **6** will help you see how you can contribute to a team even if you're not in an office. Chapter **7** offers help on coping with feelings of isolation.

Deciding whether working from home would work for *you*

For many people, working from home (sometimes known as 'teleworking') is the holy grail of employment options. In an ideal set-up, it frees you up from the strains of commuting so that you can get your work done in peace without the many interruptions of being in an office, and still have plenty of time left to pursue other interests outside work.

Having said that, making the transition to working from home isn't always smooth. For convenience, cost, and comfort, there's nothing quite like a home office, but on the minus side, you're on your own, literally—and if you're not disciplined, you'll be spending more time with the children, the pets, or in front of the fridge than working where you belong. It can take a while to settle into a routine.

There's clearly a lot to think about before you take the plunge, but make a start by thinking about the following questions:

■ Would I feel isolated if I'm at home more often than normal?

- **Could I separate business and personal life if both were under the same roof?**
- **Am I a workaholic and if so, would an office at home worsen that problem?**

Step one: Work out how susceptible you are to feelings of isolation

The basic fact is that some people are much more comfortable with their own company than others. Thinking about certain aspects of your personality will help you find out how suited you are to working from home.

Some people are natural **extroverts** and thrive on the company of others. They are motivated by the attention they receive and will look to others (consciously or subconsciously) and their reactions for direction. They are naturally warm and affectionate, trusting, and believe that others are basically good. These people may be able to work effectively from home but are likely to suffer from isolation blues. They need to have a strategy to work from home and still get the contact with the 'outside world' that they need. See chapter seven for more information on how to cope with feelings of isolation.

More **introverted** people need space and time away from others to recharge their batteries as they find social interaction quite draining. They are more internally motivated and have an inner sense of mission. They may feel suspicious of others' motives and are disinclined to believe or trust them without good reason. They're also cooler and more detached in group situations. These people are more naturally suited to maintaining their balance and motivation in an isolated environment, but they too can benefit from broadening their network to get input and support from others. Turn to chapters five and six for help on this point.

Step two: Be honest about your reasons for wanting to work at home

People choose to work from home for all sorts of reasons. There are lots of positive reasons for wanting to spend less time in the office yet still contribute to your life at work, such as growing family commitments or a decision to study part-time.

There are, however, more negative reasons that may force us to look for an escape for a few days in the week, such as:

- a difficult boss
- office politics
- bullying or harassment
- an office romance gone sour
- overwork
- work-related stress

Most people have suffered from one or several of these problems at one time or another, and it's worth trying to tackle the issue before seeing working at home as a way out. If you still want to work at home afterwards, fine, but think carefully about your motivations first. With a little courage and resolution, you'll feel 100% better if you sort things out.

If you *are* unhappy at work, remember that:

- you have the same right as others to be treated respectfully in the workplace
- you should seek help as soon as you can if you are being bullied or harassed in any way. If you feel you can't talk to your manager about this situation, tell a trusted friend, someone who works in HR, or your union representative.
- stress can make you ill and affects not only your work life, but your home life too. It's essential that you let people know how you're feeling so that they can take steps to help you. Don't be afraid to delegate to a colleague or junior member of staff if you can; delegation isn't an admission of failure, but a sign of sensible time management.
- everyone makes mistakes. It's wrong to put yourself under too much pressure to be perfect, as no-one else is! Remember that a mistake is only a mistake if you don't learn anything from it, so don't beat yourself up if things go awry at times. Let your manager know if you're worried about something, take steps to address it if you can, and then move on.

Working at home = workaholic?

If you know you have workaholic tendencies, think carefully about your work/life balance before you start working from home, as setting up a home office will mean that you can be checking your e-mail 'just in case' at all hours of the day or night. Obviously it's important to be productive at work—it's what we get paid for, after all—but you need to be sensible about things for your own sake. Chapter three is full of advice on how to put a limit on your working hours, but an essential first step is your being aware of your own limitations and of the need to balance the demands of work and other areas of your life.

Step three: Talk it through with those closest to you

If you have a partner, family, or housemates, your spending more time at home will have an impact on them too. In most cases this will be a positive one, and in fact someone else may have suggested to you that you work more flexibly; if you have family commitments, for example, you may need to work with others to make sure babies, young children, or sick relatives are looked after.

Don't just take a unilateral decision, though, and make sure that your plans don't clash with other people's to such an extent that they make your ideas unworkable. This isn't to say that you shouldn't explore this option—many couples work very successfully from home together—but just make sure that your dream scenario will work in reality.

Step four: Talk to your boss about it

Working flexibly is an important employment issue and most people agree that it can contribute positively to a good work—life balance.

As of April 2003 and under the terms of the Employment Act 2002, parents of children under the age of 6, or of less abled-bodied children under the age of 18, may request flexible working hours, but they need to have completed six months' continuous service at the company or organisation in question before making that request. Some organisations may also consider flexible working if you need to care for a dependent adult, such as your spouse, partner, or parent.

TOP TIP
Remember that *requesting* flexible working arrangements doesn't mean that you'll automatically be granted them! You need to make a good case that stresses how your new working style will benefit the business, rather than detract from it.

You don't have to be a parent to request a new working arrangement, but whatever your reasons, you have to clear it with your boss.

✔ As a first step, drop him or her a short e-mail about your plans, rather than just turning up in their office one day and firing questions at them. Unless you've had conversations on this theme before, they probably have no idea that you've been thinking about it, so a bit of advance warning will make them feel less ambushed by the whole thing.

Try to spell out the potential benefits of your working from home and plan in advance how to answer these questions:

- Do you think you will still be able be an effective team member?
- How would a change in your working hours affect your colleagues?
- What will be the overall effect on the work you do, in your view?
- How could a change in your working hours affect the business positively?

If your boss agrees to your plans, tell any colleagues or contacts who might need to know, and then you can start thinking about the logistics of setting up a home office.

Step five: Be prepared for a period of readjustment

There is a lot to think about when you're planning a new working arrangement, and setting up a home office can be a lot of fun. You have to realise, though, that there are only so many times you can come up with the world's best filing system, rehang that poster on the wall, or check to see if anyone's rung you in the last five minutes. You will have to buckle down and do some work at some point, and at first you might find it hard-going.

Don't expect to be able to settle down straightaway (although obviously it would be great if you can!)—it's very likely that you'll need to take some time to adjust. Try to make, and stick to, simple to-do lists of useful tasks to help see you through the early days.

The following chapters will take you through the key steps to a successful home office. Good luck!

Common Mistakes

✗ **You don't realise how much you miss the company of others**

If you're naturally a gregarious person, you may find it difficult to work away from the 'buzz' of the office. Obviously you'd get used to your new way of working in the end, but think long and hard about whether it's the right move for you—it's just not some people's cup of tea.

✗ You decide to work from home for the wrong reasons

If you're having a difficult time at work, the idea of retreating to the comfort of your own home can be very tempting. However, it's not a good idea if there is a real and serious problem that you need to face—you'll still have to deal with it on the days you are in the office. Remember that *no-one* has the right to treat you unfairly in the workplace, however high up the food-chain they are, and you have every right to be treated with respect. Don't stand for bullying or harassment of any kind and act quickly before your health begins to suffer. The links at the end of this chapter suggest some helpful first ports of call.

✗ You think *everyone* will see it as a good idea

While working from home might be your idea of bliss, it might not suit some of the other people affected by your decision. Talk it over with your partner and/or your family to work out some scenarios that everyone's happy with, and then talk to your boss about your plans. Explain what you want to do and take care to stress how the change in your working routine will make a positive contribution.

STEPS TO SUCCESS

✔ Be sure that you're the right type of person to spend more time away from the office. Would you be happy spending more time on your own?

✔ Be honest with yourself about your reasons for wanting to work at home. Don't do it if you're trying to avoid a problem in the workplace.

✔ If you are being treated badly at work, act quickly to resolve the problem. Letting things drag on will have a serious effect on your health and happiness.

✔ If you have workaholic tendencies, think hard about whether working from home truly is a good idea for you. At least if you're in the office you have to go home at some point!

✔ Talk through your plans with anyone who will be affected by it, such as your partner, family, or housemates. Listen to any objections or suggestions they have and remember that you can't have everything your own way all the time.

✔ Clear your plans with your boss. Break news of your plans to them sensibly and give them some warning so that your request doesn't look or sound like an ultimatum.

✔ Emphasise the benefits that your working at home for some or all of the week would bring to the company.

✔ Realise you'll need a period of adjustment when you start to work from home. Set yourself sensible to-do lists so that you achieve something while you're getting used to your new set-up.

Useful links

Department of Trade and Industry:
www.dti.gov.uk/bestpractice/people/change.htm
European Telework Online:
www.eto.org.uk/faq/faq03.htm
iVillage.co.uk:
www.ivillage.co.uk/workcareer
Telework Association:
www.tca.org.uk
Total Jobs.com:
www.totaljobs.com/editorial/getadvice_worklife/ home.shtm

Setting up your home office

If you've decided that working from home is the best option for you, you now need to make it happen. The key to success here is being realistic! You may have worked from home for the odd morning or afternoon previously and in that situation, you could probably just cope with papers being spread out all over the kitchen table or pinned up on the wall of the spare room. Working like this for any length of time will, however, drive you and your family or housemates mad. If you want other people to take you seriously, you need to take your new working set-up just as seriously and spend some time thinking about how it will all fit together.

Don't feel guilty for thinking through all your options thoroughly—you'll be spending a good deal of time in your home office, so it really will all be worth it.

Step one: Plan the layout of your office

When you're planning a home office, you need to think about where to locate it, how to decorate it, and how to furnish it. If you're going to work from home because you've decided to start your own business, the office is even more important, as it'll be the hub of your new enterprise. Some people even make a scale drawing of the room they intend to use, then place to-scale furniture on it to decide on the best layout. You could also take the advice of office-ware stockists — many of the larger retailers offer an office-planning service.

TOP TIP

If you've a good eye and are handy with a computer, you could also use some software to help you plan your layout well. See the useful links at the end of this chapter for a suggestion.

First of all, think about which room in your home could best be used as, or converted into, an office. Make sure that the room you choose:

- has enough light for you to be able to work comfortably
- has enough space for you to be able to store any relevant equipment and paperwork
- is equipped so that you can use your phone and computer
- is comfortable temperature-wise. You'll never get anything done if you're too cold or too hot — it's hard to concentrate on anything other than how uncomfortable you're feeling otherwise — so make the sure the room has the right amount of heating and/or ventilation for you.

TOP TIP

Try, as far as you can, not to work in a dark room. While you can, obviously, boost the level of light with lamps, it can be very depressing to work in a dimly-lit space, especially in the winter months. A brighter space, with plenty of natural light, will boost your spirits and keep you motivated.

Step two: Make sure you're comfortable and that you have the right equipment

Office décor is important. It needs to be functional, but that doesn't mean it has to be boring or austere—you'll work much better in a room that you actually enjoy spending time in.

You don't have to spend a fortune, but choose good lighting, paint/wallpaper, floor covering and so on—or work in a room that has all of these already—so that your office is a good place to be.

Besides getting the right atmosphere, think about the communications side of things: how do you want to contact others? And can people contact you? Check whether you need to run more phone lines and electrical sockets into the room to support the office equipment.

TOP TIP

It might be worth investigating the cost of having an extra phone line, or a dedicated business phone line, installed. This will help keep work and home calls separate, which would be a big help if someone else is likely to be at home at the same time as you. Your phone company will be able to give you an idea of the costs involved; you may have to pay a quarterly cost for an extra service on top of any installation charges.

Your basic package of office equipment will depend on what industry you work in and what your level of activity is, but it will probably include:

- desk
- chair
- computer(s) and peripherals
- software
- phones and phone service for voice, fax, and Internet
- scanner or separate copier
- filing cabinet
- shredder, if you have confidential information and documents to dispose of

If you're running your own business, you might want to invest in a digital camera so that you can put photos of your products on a website.

If you're planning to use the office for a small business, the Inland Revenue will allow you to deduct certain expenses connected to the business. For that reason, the office must be completely dedicated to the business and not merely a spare bedroom with a fold-up desk and your cordless phone! Good record keeping is very important if you plan to deduct expenses and part of the mortgage interest, utilities, and phone bills for business activity. Visit the IR's website (given in the Useful Links section at the end of this chapter) for more information.

✔ Upgrade your connection to the Internet, if at all possible, so that you have a broadband connection. This option isn't available in all areas but if you can upgrade, it'll mean that you can work more quickly and effectively and be easier to contact too, as you'll be able to keep your phone lines free. Your phone company's website should be able to tell you whether broadband is available in your area; you're normally asked to enter your postcode into a search box in the relevant section.

TOP TIP
**A broadband connection is a life-saver if your
type of work means that you need to send or
receive large files from colleagues and
contacts—without it, you'll spend hours**

waiting for the files to download. Another good way of cutting down on this waiting-time is to ask people to 'zip' files that they send to you, which means that the file size is compressed and so they can be sent and received much more quickly. WinZip is a popular software package that allows you to do just that, and a single user licence costs roughly £20.

Finally, don't forget that you'll need some basic office supplies—pens, paper, Post-it® notes, stapler, scissors, highlighter pens, and so on.

TOP TIP
The sort of investment you'll need to kit out your home office will, of course, depend on the type of work you do. If you have a computer already, you'll have saved on the greatest outlay, but if you don't have one, allow between £1,000 and £3,000 for your total budget. Make a list and work out what you can afford beforehand. This is especially useful if you're starting your own business, as you don't want to blow your entire savings on setting up the office, and then have nothing to spend on attracting customers.

Step three: Think about ergonomics

I Understand the benefits

Why do you need to bother with ergonomics? Because they're not a management fad, but a method of adapting equipment and surroundings so that you can work as efficiently as possible. The main aim is to create a safe, comfortable, and stress-reduced environment, which sounds like just what you need when you're working from home.

In most workplaces, workstations are assessed to make sure that they are ergonomic and if you choose to work from home full or part-time, someone from your office may come and check whether your home working space conforms to the recommended standards. If not, it's worth making some checks for yourself. It may sound like one more thing to worry about that you just don't have time for, but it is worth being sensible—it will cut down on the risk of problems such as RSI, for example. Some simple actions to take include:

✔ using a good-quality, adjustable chair to help avoid back problems

✔ using an ergonomic mouse to reduce strain on the wrists and lower arm muscles

✔ using a keyboard with palm rests

2 Make yourself comfortable

Having a good chair is essential when you're spending a lot of time working at your desk. To make sure you're sitting comfortably:

✔ adjust the backrest and armrests of your chair so that you sit in an upright position and don't slouch. The backrest should follow the natural 'S' curve of your spine.

✔ lower or raise the height of the chair so that your wrists, hands, and forearms are horizontal with the desk

✔ place your feet flat on the floor or use a footrest if you prefer

✔ keep your head up and your shoulders relaxed

✔ remove any obstacles beneath your desk that prevent you from being able to fit your legs and feet underneath comfortably

3 Watch out for eye strain

Many people get tired or sore eyes from working at their computer for much of the day. To help cut down on any discomfort:

✔ make sure your computer monitor is at a comfortable distance from your eyes

✔ allow enough space on the desk to rest your hands and
  wrists, so that you can keep movement of the wrists to a
  minimum

✔ adjust the brightness and colour contrast of your
  computer screen and make sure it is reflection-free and
  clean

✔ avoid long periods of repetitive activity; for example,
  alternate computer-based work with other tasks, such
  as filing, telephoning, or reading

✔ if you spend a lot of time doing close work, such as
  checking contracts, make sure you have enough light
  to read by

4 Keep it tidy!

When you choose a desk or recycle a table from elsewhere
in the house to use as your desk, make sure it's big enough
for you to work comfortably, as mentioned above, and also
that it leaves you enough room to spread out the pieces of
paper, books, or other equipment that you need.

Whatever you do, try not to 'store' things on the floor; it's not
only dangerous, but clutter will soon build up and make the
office look like an uninviting bomb site. File things when
you can and check through piles of paper regularly, being
ruthless about what you can throw away, recycle, or shred
if appropriate.

TOP TIP
Don't worry too much about throwing away
something important by accident. If
the document really is that important,
it will come back to you one way or
another at a future date.

Step four: Think about insurance

I Buildings and contents insurance

The majority of people who work from home tend to have
reasonably sedentary desk-based tasks to do. If, however,
your field of expertise or new business venture involves the
manufacture or repair of goods, you should check that your
existing buildings and contents insurance will cover your
business activities too.

2 Computer insurance

Computer insurance may be worth investigating if you
don't have it already. Most policies cover you for
breakdowns and loss of information, but check that your
cover includes the computer environment, including e-mail
and Internet access system. Different types of machinery
insurance polices are available to cover breakdown and
inspection cover.

TOP TIP

Ask your company's computer helpdesk or resident techie to set up remote e-mail access for you, so that you can read all e-mails sent to your work account while you're at home. If this isn't possible, leave an out-of-office message on your work e-mail with your home e-mail details on it and/or your phone number, so that people can contact you that way. This will make sure that vital tasks don't get missed while you're out of the office.

Step five: Check it all works!

Just think how frustrating it would be if, on your first day of working from home, nothing works: your computer won't boot up, you can't use your Internet connection, and you've lost all your pens and paper to take down a vital phone message.

To spare yourself all this stress, do a test run on a day agreed with your colleagues so that you can sort out any problems that arise well in advance. This will be particularly useful if you're working from home full-time or for a good proportion of the week. It will also give you a chance to set up a routine for your home working; see Chapter 3 for more information on this.

TOP TIP

If you do a lot of work on computer when you're working at home, remember that you won't have the back-up systems in place there that you rely on at the office. Save your work frequently and use the automatic save functions that many software packages offer; you can set these to save your work every few minutes so that if the worst comes to the worst and your computer crashes, you don't have to start everything from scratch.

Common mistakes

✗ You only go halfway with the office arrangement

Starting a home office on the dining-room table isn't a good idea, and neither is committing only half-heartedly to making a guestroom into a real office. If you don't treat the office seriously, there's a better than even chance you won't take your work seriously either. Carve out a separate space and dedicate it as the office; you'll feel better and your work will benefit from that decision.

STEPS TO SUCCESS

✔ Don't feel guilty about spending time planning the layout of your office; you'll be spending a lot of time there, so it's really important that you find a space that works for you.

✓ Make sure your office has plenty of natural light. Working in a dark space can be depressing and may have a negative impact on your mood and motivation.

✓ Check that you have enough room in your office to work comfortably and to store all relevant paperwork and equipment.

✓ Think about the ergonomics of your office; is everything arranged so that it's functional but comfortable?

✓ Keep your office tidy! Don't use the floor as a storage space. It's not only dangerous to litter the floor with piles of paper or empty boxes, but you'll make the office a place that you don't want to visit. Check through all your paperwork regularly and recycle what you don't need.

✓ Make sure that you can contact people easily, and that they can contact you.

✓ Check that you've enough phone points and upgrade your Internet connection to broadband if you can. This will mean you can download files much more quickly and also that you can send e-mails or work online and still take or make phone calls.

✓ If you're working from home because you've set up a new business, work out a budget carefully and stick to it.

✔ Make sure your insurance is up-to-date and that it covers any new equipment you're using in your home office.

✔ Try to arrange remote access to your office e-mail if at all possible for the days you're working at home. This will mean that you don't return to a flood of urgent messages when you're back at the office.

✔ Back up frequently all work you do on your computer at home.

✔ Do a test run before you launch yourself into your new working regime. This will let you iron out any problems or unforeseen hitches.

Useful links

Entrepreneur
www.entrepreneur.com
Facility Planning Software:
www.smartdraw.com/specials/
facilityplanning.asp?id=15528
Go Home:
www.gohome.com
Inland Revenue:
www.inlandrevenue.gov.uk/menus/b_taxpayers.htm
Setting up a home office:
www.money.guardian.co.uk/advicebank/
planyourworkinglife

Getting used to working from home

As we found out in the last chapter, working from home has become much easier over recent years, especially as technology has become more sophisticated. Some people, especially those who have been used to working in larger companies, can take a while to get used to working in a less structured setting. This chapter offers some advice on how to get the best from working at home.

Step one: Create some boundaries

As we said in Chapter 1, when you start working from home, it's crucial that you set up a suitable work environment and set boundaries. It's hopeless trying to balance your laptop on your knee in the kitchen while you attempt to avoid intrusions from family or friends; you need to set rules for yourself and others so that everyone can support your efforts rather than sabotage them.

If there are other people at home, be clear about the time you set aside for working. Non-work interruptions can be frustrating when you're trying to get something done to a deadline.

✔ Set up boundaries by establishing in advance how you're going to manage your time at home, including things like the beginning and ending of your working day. Having a separate room to work in is key here as you can close the door and cut down on disturbances. Stick to your guns and people will soon get the message.

✔ If your work requires you to receive visitors, try to find an area where they won't be distracted by your domestic arrangements. Having to ignore the pile of washing on the kitchen floor can be very off-putting, however friendly you are with your guests. If you're unable to avoid these situations, find a local hotel or restaurant where you can meet for an hour or two. Again, this is about creating boundaries that will enable you to maintain focus and create an impression of professionalism.

TOP TIP

If you're an extrovert and enjoy the buzz of having other people around, it's important to recognise and cater for this. You could try planning a certain number of days in the office and balance these with quieter, more productive days at home. If you're self-employed, you may need to schedule visits and meetings sufficiently regularly for you to feel involved with and energised by others.

Step two: Get into a routine

It's important to differentiate your day between being 'at work' and 'at home'. If your working and resting times become confused, it can feel as if you're always on duty, and when you *do* take a break you can feel guilty that you aren't finishing a project. This differentiation comes naturally when you have to travel to and from work, but when your routine changes you'll need to find a way to make this shift yourself. For example, it could be signalled by a routine; making a cup of coffee, taking it to your desk, closing your door, and switching on the computer. Once you've done this a few times, this routine creates the boundary within which you can work effectively.

TOP TIP

Although the idea of wandering into your office pyjama-clad may appeal, get up and get dressed as if you were going into the office. Obviously you don't have to wear a suit or very smart clothes, but getting changed is another 'signal' that you're starting your working day .

✔ Plan your day so that you don't find yourself wasting time. The advantage of working from home is that you have greater control over interruptions. People will no longer be able to wander past your desk at will and ask you for some information or, worse, to do something for them. A great deal of time is wasted in these 'Oh, by the way . . .' moments that happen mostly because you're accessible or visible.

Step three: Take regular breaks

✔ Make sure you take breaks throughout the day. Most people's concentration starts to diminish after about twenty minutes, and if you continue to work after this time thinking can become a struggle. Taking a break, perhaps a short walk, can re-energise your thinking capability. Of course, breaks need to be balanced by the need to be productive.

✔ Try not to get distracted by picking up something else that needs doing. You'll only end up wasting time and lowering your efficiency by spreading your energies too thinly.

Step four: Work at your work—life balance

✔ Make sure you plan for the end of the day as well. When you work at home, it's all too easy to stay sitting in your workspace well into the evening and to ignore the private side of your life. It can be hard to juggle these two aspects of your life, but everyone needs a break from work.

TOP TIP
**Make some time for yourself, friends, family,
and other interests; you'll be much
happier in the long term .**

Find out about your tax status

If your decision to work at home is linked to a decision to
work for yourself, you'll find that having an office in the
home may qualify you for tax concessions. Tax relief is
available on your mortgage interest, heating, and
telephone bills, and the cost of capital equipment and
services needed to support your business. The Inland
Revenue or your accountant will guide you on what tax
benefits you may receive. Anyone starting a new business
must register with the Inland Revenue within a strict time
period, so visit their website (details below) for full
information. You may also need to register for VAT too,
depending on what your income will be. The figure tends
to change each year with the Budget, so contact your
local VAT registration office for advice or find more
information at **www.hmce.gov.uk**. (HM Customs and
Excise has responsibility for collecting VAT revenue,
rather than the Inland Revenue.)

Common mistakes

✗ You lose your focus

For those who enjoy dynamic environments and the cut
and thrust of being in a busy office, working from home
may not be enjoyable. It's tempting for this type of
person to create dynamism for themselves by finding
activities that distract them from his or her own
company. Flitting around from task to task can create a
feeling of being 'in the flow', but may not be very
productive. If you worry that you may be prone to finding
'displacement' activities rather than doing any work,
spend a few minutes at the beginning of the day creating
a 'to do' list. This will focus your energy and make sure
that there's a valuable output to the day's activities.

✗ You can't switch off

It's very easy for people to work beyond the call of duty
when the office is located in the home. This is especially
the case if you've started a new business; the first stages
can be really hectic and long hours are often
unavoidable. 'I'll just go and answer a few e-mails . . .'
can become a lengthy session in front of the computer
that eats into private time. Try to discipline yourself to
keep to the 'rules' that you've set, with only occasional
exceptions for real emergencies or key deadlines.

✗ You lose track of the time

If you miss the energy you get from working with others,
you might turn to the phone as a substitute for their

presence around you. It's easy to pass a lot of the day on the phone and to find that, as a result, you have to work late to actually achieve anything that day. Again, this is a question of discipline. Give yourself time to be in touch with others, but keep control of it. A large clock on the wall in front of you is a good reminder of how long you're spending on each activity!

STEPS TO SUCCESS

✔ Create some boundaries between your work space and your home space so that you and separate the two halves of your life more easily.

✔ Make some simple rules, such as what will be the beginning and end times of your working day so that you and anyone who lives with you can get used to your new routine.

✔ Keep your work space tidy and welcoming so that any visitors to your home office won't be alarmed by your domestic arrangements!

✔ Plan your day so that you actually get something done. Make sure you also take regular breaks throughout the day, though, as they will help you keep your concentration up.

✔ Don't let yourself get distracted by household or garden chores that need doing. They can wait until you've got some work done.

✔ If you're an extrovert and benefit from having other people around, don't cut yourself off. Balance time in the office with quieter time at home so that you have the best of both worlds.

✔ Switch off in all senses at the end of the day. Keep to your rules and end your work day when you planned to. Don't keep rushing off to check your e-mail during the evening unless there's a genuine emergency or important deadline to deal with.

Useful links

Homeworking.com:
www.homeworking.com
Inland Revenue:
www.inlandrevenue.gov.uk
iVillage.co.uk:
**www.ivillage.co.uk/workcareer/worklife/balnews/
articles/0,,206_178116,00.html**

4 Learning to prioritise tasks

Keeping control of tasks is an essential skill to master, and one that's particularly useful if you decide to work from home. Good prioritisation helps you to avoid distraction and to become more efficient and self-reliant.

Some people naturally like structure in their life: control is one of the 'big five' personality factors that psychologists agree on. If being in control is important to you and you enjoy structure, order, and routines, it's unlikely that you'll struggle with the steps laid out below.

If, on the other hand, you prefer freedom and variety, you may feel constrained by structure and routines and find it harder to follow these steps. Persevere if you can, as you'll really reap some benefits. It might be a good idea to concentrate on using Step one, so that you're at least clear about what you're trying to achieve with your efforts. Learning to prioritise frees up a lot of time for whatever you would prefer to be doing. Use the steps below as a framework and schedule imaginatively, to give you the variety you need in your daily life.

Step one: Decide on your objectives

If you start off by being clear about what you want to achieve, the chances are that you'll succeed brilliantly. There are several levels to this step. Ask yourself:

- What do you (personally) want to get out of any particular period of work (say a month, six months)?
- What do your boss/team/clients/company need you to achieve during this time?
- What specific goals do you want to have achieved by the end of this month?

✔ Write the answers to these questions on a sheet of A4. Hang them in a prominent place in your office, ideally where a distracted eye will fall. You can add on an adjacent sheet of A4 your objectives for your life outside work, if you feel inclined to.

You'll probably have several answers for each question, because our objectives are usually plural. If this is the case, you'll need to identify the *relative* importance of each element of your answer; it may help to organise your page with the most important elements first. Next to these will be the answers to the following questions, which it will become habitual to write at the beginning of the working week and day.

- What do you need to get done by the end of this week?
- What do you need to get done today?

The answers to these simple questions will guide you through the chaos of each day. When faced with requests or demands for your time and attention, ask yourself how they'll help you towards your objectives:

■ Should I do it now or after more important objectives have been met?
■ Is this something I need to deal with today?
■ Is this something I need to deal with this week?
■ Do I need to sort it out this month?
■ Can this go right on the end of my list, to do if I have time?
■ Should I bother with this at all?
■ Can I delegate this to someone else?

Step two: Use tools to help you

Although you don't want to clutter up your life even further, there are some tools that can help you live according to your priorities.

Diary

A diary helps you to plan ahead, appropriately scheduling specific dates or times for tasks and actions. It helps you to structure time towards deadlines so that you can monitor interim goals more easily and make sure they're met, with your ultimate goal being to deliver the outcome you want on time.

✔ Divide projects and objectives into constituent parts and place 'milestones' in your diary. Don't forget to schedule time to meet people, or you could risk isolating yourself.

A diary is especially useful to structure your time if you have lots of short meetings or telephone calls or if you need long chunks of time to focus on difficult, complex, or creative work. By communicating your need to your colleagues and concentrating meetings and other work into one section of the day or week, you free yourself to work in a more effective manner.

Diaries now come in the traditional paper format, in software for your PC or notebook such as Microsoft Outlook or in new '3G' formats as part of a mobile gadget with multiple functions. While computerised devices may offer useful features to those who learn how to use them, a paper diary does the job and is unlikely to develop technical trouble, run out of power or be incompatible with other systems.

To-do list

In its simplest form, a To-do list is a place to record the things you need to do, so that you can tick them off as you achieve them. Software that allows you to add priorities, due dates, and reminders is readily available, for PCs, notebooks, or for phones and other mobile devices. Again, the extra features may be nice to have but a simple paper list is fine.

If you're aware that you take on too many tasks, a To-do list may help you to visualise your workload and manage requests more assertively. Always keep your objectives in mind when you're writing your To-do list.

✔ Next to each entry on your list give the task a number to reflect the priority of the task relative to your objectives and the other tasks. You can even make your list public so that your boss and colleagues can see the work already assigned and do some of the prioritising for you.

Time audit

This is a backwards look at how you've been spending your time. It's a useful tool to monitor how well you're focusing your time on the objectives you want to achieve.

✔ Looking back through your diary and To-do list, estimate the amount of time that you spent working towards the objectives you set yourself. Do the same for your time and objectives outside work. How does your time allocation tally? What needs to change: your objectives and priorities or your time management?

Project planner

When managing projects, a project planning system can help you to break down a complex system easily into its constituent elements, identify milestones, assign tasks to others and keep track of progress. This can be done on paper, whiteboard, or flipcharts or on a PC or notebook using one of the software tools on the market.

TOP TIP

'Prioritise' is a verb. That means action, not tools. People can have a very fancy toolkit to help them but it has no effect until they use it. Don't fool yourself that having a diary and a To-do list means that you're organised. Even filling them in will not help alone. It's the discipline of following the schedule in your diary and focusing on the completion of each task on the To-do list that will make you efficient and successful.

Step three: Manage your inputs and outputs

The process of working efficiently comes in managing the inputs as they happen and remaining focused on the output of the most important and urgent task.

First and most important: be clear which set of objectives you should be focussed upon now—work or home objectives. If you work from home, separate your work space from your home space as far as you can. Separate work time from home time, work phone line from home phone line, and home e-mail from work e-mail too. This way you can protect yourself from the stress of role confusion.

Managing output

Here is a checklist of things to do when you start your work time:

✓ Look up at your objectives on the wall to focus you on what you're achieving.

✓ Look at your diary and see what you've scheduled and how much time you have spare.

✓ Look at your To-do list and pick out the tasks that are the most important and urgent. You can choose to start a long task and finish it on a different day or you may prefer to pick a single task that will fit within the time you have available.

✓ Allow yourself time for interruptions and three or four 10-minute breaks and a longer meal break within a working day. You'll be more focussed and effective if you stay fresh. Now you can write your objectives for the day.

Managing input

✓ Make your days more efficient by allocating time slots to post, e-mails, and incoming phone calls.

How you do this will depend on your role, but for most people the post will only need attention once a day.

✓ Sort out your post near the bin, making three piles:

- junk. No pile for this: straight into the bin.
- items to file for reference: put them away directly after opening everything
- items to deal with immediately: respond to each one quickly and efficiently
- items requiring more attention: add to your To-do list or schedule specific time in your diary. Don't forget to think about how important the item is to the achievement of your objectives.

E-mails carry the expectation that they'll be seen and dealt with immediately and some may generate more interruptions if left too long. On the other hand, very few roles require that people need to respond to each e-mail as it arrives.

✔ Turn off your message alert as it will distract you each time you get a new message and allocate a maximum of three slots in the day for responding to e-mail. Early morning mail may be urgent, so start the day with a quick check, check again after lunch and do a final check as you finish work for the day. Use the same 'three-piles-plus-the-bin' system as you did with your post.

How you deal with your phones depends on your role. You may be expected to answer immediately during office hours. Perhaps you prefer to have the variety of contact with others throughout the day and enjoy the social side of the interruption. Some calls may be quickly dealt with if answered immediately, saving yourself and others time.

✔ If your role allows it, try to switch on the answerphone and return calls during allocated slots through the day, as with e-mails. If this system is acceptable, it does allow you greater focus on your objectives for the day, making you more productive. This does require you to get into the habit of regularly checking and returning calls.

TOP TIP

Whatever your line of work, try not to put off 'horrible' jobs. They'll have to be done at some point, and it's a good idea to tackle them early in the day. That way, you'll have feel as if you've accomplished something within just a short time of starting work and you'll also be able to concentrate better on other tasks, as you'll no longer be worrying about the job you'd been dreading.

Common mistakes

✗ **You confuse housework with work**
Part of the beauty of working from home may be the flexibility. But don't fool yourself that you're working if you are in fact fixing things around the house or doing the washing. Restrict these activities to before work, after work, or during a lunch break.

✗ **Your standards drop over time**
You owe it to yourself to put in a full and focussed day towards your objectives or it's unlikely that you'll meet

them. If it helps, imagine your boss or colleague's reaction to a piece of work you're finishing. Does it do you justice?

STEPS TO SUCCESS

✔ Know what you're trying to achieve. Bringing abstract, large, or vague objectives into current targets by breaking them down into smaller and more manageable chunks makes them more achievable. If you have trouble doing this, get help from your boss or a business coach.

✔ Keep the correct set of objectives in mind at all times.

✔ Know your tools and how to use them. If in doubt about the technology, work a dual system approach until you're certain that you can rely upon it.

✔ Build your own way of managing inputs and outputs based upon the suggestions in this section into your routine. Have a schedule that helps you and stick to it.

✔ Be clear about your different roles and try to keep them separate. There will be times when you're required to switch between them but don't allow this to become routine.

✔ If you find you're slipping back into your old haphazard methods, return to this section regularly to remind yourself. If you struggle at first, have faith! Anyone can learn to prioritise but it may take some time for it to become habitual.

Useful links

BBC Learning:
**www.bbc.co.uk/learning/returning/learninglives/time/
c_prioritising_01.shtml**
Mind Tools:
www.mindtools.com/page5.html
Time Management Training Skills and Tips:
www.tsuccess.dircon.co.uk/timemanagementtips.htm

Maintaining your relationships with the office and key contacts

Why is the maintenance of a working network so important? Because whether you're working alone at home or in a busy office, you'll need a network around you to get things done. It's also easy to feel isolated if you don't maintain regular contact with others, as we'll see in Chapter 7.

Remember that:

- your network may offer *inputs*: by gathering, processing and passing on information to you; by procuring services or items required for your work; by sharing insight, ideas, opportunities, and expertise with you.
- your network may also provide *outputs*: by doing work that you delegate; by passing on information to others; by making decisions that help you to proceed.

When you're working at home you're all the more likely to need a strong network to be as effective as you can in your work. If you spend time looking after your work relationships, you'll be protecting yourself against some of the downsides of being out of the office for some or all of the week.

Step one: Think about your current key contacts

Take a clean sheet of paper and draw a Mind Map® to identify the main groups of key contacts that you maintain in order to perform your everyday work.

For example:

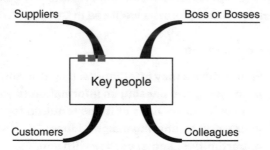

Step two: Think about who your future key contacts might be

Now, using a different colour, identify the kind of contacts that could be helpful to you in the future. The idea is to list groups with the *potential* to help, rather than just those you are sure will help you. As you can see below, the number of branches on the map quickly increases and this is before you've even started to list the various individuals under each branch.

For example:

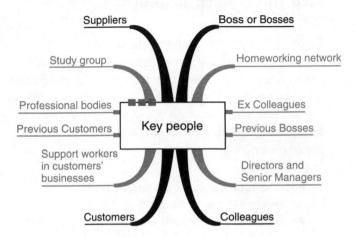

The network represented by the black arrows represents your main contact group and the people with whom you're in most regular contact. The network represented by the blue arrows is the one that you need to build.

TOP TIP

It's best to create and work at building your network before you need it to help you out. Well connected people often seem to be more 'lucky' than others are; they frequently seem to be in the right place at the right time. In fact, what they've done is to work hard at making those connections which could to the big assignment, important new customer, or dream job they've been looking for.

Step three: Keep in touch!

1 Think about the best way to do it

As discussed in Chapter 2, there are many ways to make getting in touch easy. These can range from a simple phone call, to an e-mail, to a text message. What works best? Well, it depends on you, the person you want to contact, and what you want talk to them about. Here are some rough guidelines, though:

- **Face-to-face**: best method for delegating a project, delivering performance feedback and for negotiation
- **Phone calls**: great when you expect lots of back and forth interaction or need answers fast
- **Instant messaging**: can simulate a conversation and be carried on in the background, much in the same way that office chat takes place in an open plan environment.
- **E-mail**: good for collaboration on attached files, nice when you want to refer to a record of your 'conversation' and very useful for global interactions, where time differences make phone contact difficult.

2 Think about when and how often to contact others

Your current network is clearly a priority and you'll have the details of those people close to hand, so it's a good idea to start there. For each person you need to decide what you're going to do to maintain the relationship and how frequently, but it's a good idea to follow this general pattern:

✔ make contact

✔ keep it genuine

✔ keep it short

✔ make it a habit

Keeping in contact isn't supposed to be a chore, so as well as phone calls or online chats, take a break from the same old-same old and think about meeting for:

- breakfast meeting
- coffee
- lunch or dinner
- drinks at a pub or bar
- a day out at a sporting event
- a visit to a theatre or show

TOP TIP
Maintain your relationships carefully and don't be selfish. If you only contact people when you want something, you'll create an 'uh-oh' effect when you call. Relationships need oiling in between times to ensure they are ready, rather than rusty, when you need them. Always ask others if there's anything *you* can do to help *them*.

The easiest relationships to maintain are those that are based upon genuine and comfortable interactions between individuals.

✔ Try to identify ways of making the other person feel comfortable and confident when they talk with you. This doesn't mean using the shallow compliments of sales patter. Learning and paying attention to what is important to the other will make a big difference to the relationship that you build.

With the contacts that you have already, you'll have to make greater effort to make sure that the rapport you've already built doesn't fade. Now that you're out-of-sight in your home office, this means short but regular contact, with occasional face-to-face contact when you can. Make a point of attending office socials, such as launch events, Christmas parties, team lunches, or drinks.

With new contacts, actively building the relationship with people is critical. Although it may seem obvious, this is where people often fall down when they're trying to increase their network—if you meet a new contact, swap business cards and never do anything about it, your network will never grow. Be proactive instead. Contact people after a few days with a simple note or e-mail and then arrange to meet up after a month or so—you'll be much more likely to develop a relationship from the initial meeting.

TOP TIP
**If you decide to phone someone to keep up
your contact, it's really useful to be able
to refer to what you've said in previous
conversations. Being able to refer to the
content of your previous calls is a great
help here. Taking notes after each
contact to jog your memory later will
help to create trust and rapport
between you and your contact and
give an excellent impression.**

Common mistakes

✗ You rely on too few contacts

Reliance on too few contacts may mean that they
become exhausted. Make sure that you spread
requests for help and that you make the interaction truly
two-way.

✗ You deluge your contacts with junk mail

If the only contact you have with someone is the jokes
you send them by e-mail, you have no relationship at all.
When you finally try to contact them for real, you may find
that they've banned contact from your e-mail address to
reduce the junk in their mailbox.

Working as part of a virtual team

Working as part of a virtual team is obviously something you need to think about if you decide to work from home. In very broad strokes, a virtual team is a group of people who use a range of technologies to collaborate from different work bases. Members of a virtual team may all work for the same company, be a mix of employees and freelances, or be entirely freelance. Team members may be scattered across one country or all around the world.

Virtual teams are becoming more common as businesses open up offices around the world to expand their reach but, in attempts to keep time and cost investments to a minimum, colleagues and team members remain physically isolated from each other.

Although tele- and videoconferencing technology and other forms of electronic communication have improved greatly over the last ten years, they're poor substitutes for the chemistry that teams create as they work together, getting the best from each person's strengths and characteristics. Building and working in a successful virtual team is a great new skill to add to your bow, and one that can add

even more positive aspects to your decision to work from home.

Step one: Think about the qualities needed for an effective virtual team

An effective virtual team has the same qualities as a team working in close proximity. Good virtual team members are:

- collaborative in their work. They share information, knowledge, ideas, views, and experiences in order for the team to pull together as a unit.
- trusting of each other. Each member needs to know that the others will meet their promises promptly without personal agendas getting in the way.
- attentive to communication. Each member has to agree priorities and communicate progress regularly. There should be no withholding of information. Good communication only happens when every member takes responsibility for being part of the team and is committed to the team's purpose.
- skilled at building relationships. In the absence of actual face-to-face meetings, the development of strong, trusting relationships will depend even more than usual upon excellent communication.
- agreed on how they'll work together. All team members should agree on ground rules, written down or not, governing how they operate.

✔ Set boundaries around tasks and agree timescales. Decide collectively how the team will deal with failures to meet its objectives. You may need to call emergency meetings to create contingency plans, set new timescales, or realign the team's objectives.

✔ Agree how regularly you'll check in with each other. These reviews are designed primarily to make sure that all projects are on track, but they'll also act as early-warning systems if something is beginning to go wrong. These sessions are really important, so everyone needs to be committed to taking part in them.

✔ Discuss the possibility of conflict and decide how you'll deal with this. Many people hate even the thought of conflict and tend to ignore the possibility until it actually emerges and needs to be dealt with. Conflict isn't always a negative experience; if it's handled well and sensitively, it can clear the air and be positive in the long run.

TOP TIP
If you're working from home for most of the week and you're feeling very isolated, try using some of the virtual group technologies that are available to boost your feelings of 'belonging'. Each of these packages has different attributes, so you may want to try a few before finding one that suits you. The technologies create a way of collecting information, advice, guidance, and war stories that bring a human element to your

---

interaction. They also create a sense of team identification, because you have to be a member to have access to them. If you go to **www.google.com** and put in the keywords: 'virtual teams', 'virtual groups', or 'egroups', you'll find lots of information about available technologies.

Step four: Make electronic systems work for you

New electronic communication systems are being developed all the time, many of which can help virtual teams work well. Most people are familiar with tele- and videoconferencing as a way of bringing people together, and of course there are also the mobile phone, fax, and e-mail. There are some other useful technologies that can help people who are based far apart to communicate, though, including:

■ Web conferencing. This technology enables members of the team to sit at their respective computers and watch the meeting host illustrate his or her message on the screen. This technological aid requires access to two telephone lines, one for the telephone and one for the web connection (unless you have broadband), but is otherwise easy to set up and use.
■ document storage/sharing. There are a number of online document storage providers that enable team members

to store, edit, and access common documents. This prevents the need to create multiple versions of the same document; team members can simply work on the sections they need.

■ group e-mail. The ability to send e-mail to one or every member of the team greatly enhances the team's ability to communicate.

■ message boards. Message or bulletin boards enable group members to go to a central place where communication can take place and information is stored.

Step five: Celebrate success

It's all too easy for dispersed teams to forget to celebrate their achievements, but it's important to mark the attainment of goals. Celebration allows you to release tension, enjoy your success, and move on to the next challenge.

✔ Organise a video conference and agree to hold a virtual party. Although this may feel a little contrived, it nonetheless allows a form of togetherness and mutual appreciation. It also invites humour as you review what went well and what didn't, so it's a great way of letting things go and getting them into perspective.

Step six: Learn from the experience

T.S. Eliot wrote: 'It is possible to have the experience yet miss the meaning.' If you don't learn, you don't develop and grow. Take time to reflect on how you took your part in the team and what you've learned about yourself from doing so. What would you do differently or better next time?

Common mistakes

✗ You don't build up rapport and trust

Not spending enough time on building rapport and trust will sabotage any team, but it's a definite no-no for a virtual team. It's easy to assume that everyone has the same high level of commitment to the team's formation and purpose as the co-ordinator or team leader, but if you're a leader you need to check that everyone does feel like that, and if you're a team member, you need the chance to tell someone if you're worried about or disheartened by something. Give team members an opportunity to get to know each other so that they can work out how their talents and skills will work together to reach your objectives. This means either a physical team-building meeting or a series of virtual gatherings.

✗ You communicate badly

Forgetting to communicate with virtual colleagues is one of the main reasons that virtual teams fail. In the absence of physical proximity and the ability to pass quick messages or information over a cup of coffee in the office, out of sight can quickly become out of mind. Be sure to schedule regular meetings—and hold them without fail.

✗ You don't establish clear understanding of roles and expectations

It's important that all members understand both their role in the team and the expectations that the team leader and the members have of each other. It's too easy to assume that this is obvious. If you're the team leader, you need to be crystal-clear about this from the outset or the team will disintegrate into conflict.

Useful links

Wally Bock:
www.bockinfo.com/docs/virteam.htm
globalchange.com:
www.globalchange.com/vteams.htm
Guardian Unlimited:
**www.guardian.co.uk/online/story/
0,3605,1098799,00.html**

Coping with feelings of isolation

When people switch from working in an office to working from home, they often find that they miss the social side of working life. The natural contacts of the daily commute, bumping into friends in the kitchen, and the general banter of office life perhaps with lunches or after-work activities may be things you're happy to give up in practice, but how will you cope with the *reality* of working from home?

Step one: Use some tools to keep you in contact with others

Even if you're someone who likes their own company, it can be lonely to spend a lot of the day or the week on your own. It's important to keep in touch with colleagues when you work from home for all sorts of reasons, but even more so if you get a boost from being in touch with others. The key here is ease of connection.

✔ Start by making sure people can contact you easily when they want to. Some suggestions are given below. Obviously you don't need to implement *all* of them, but the more connection methods you have and the easier you make contact, the more likely people are to take the trouble to get in touch and keep in touch:

- reliable telephone line
- separate home and business telephone lines
- answer phone with a friendly message encouraging people to leave a message
- broadband Internet connection so that phone calls can be taken while you're online
- reliable, fast Internet service provider
- e-mail account
- e-mail signature that includes contact information, so that every message reminds people of the other ways they can get in contact
- mobile phone that receives a good signal at home
- voicemail on the mobile phone with a friendly message
- regular contacts given correct telephone number and e-mail address to use
- instant messaging available
- webcam and videoconferencing software set up and ready to use
- your entire contact network updated with your contact details at least once a year

---

TOP TIP
Make some noise! For some people, lack of
noise in their environment is a constant
reminder that they are alone. If you're
not enjoying birdsong from the
garden and find the silence a little
too deafening, putting on some

**low-key music or turning on the radio
for background noise can be a
good addition to your home office.**

Step two: Make the most of 'socials'

Even though you may have moved out of an office environment, it's a good idea to attend relevant training sessions to boost your skills or just keep in the loop. Similarly, if your employing organisation is in a state of flux, make sure you attend meetings about major changes that are taking place so that you're in touch with your colleagues and they remember that you're affected by potential rejigging too.

Keeping in touch doesn't have to be a chore, and social events are a great way of staying visible.

✔ Go to all events you're invited to, such as the Christmas party, product launches, and leaving dos. At these events in particular, you've a perfect opportunity to introduce yourself to new members of the team in a relaxed situation.

This will mean that staff turnover doesn't contribute to any feelings of isolation you may have.

✔ Take responsibility for staying in contact in between social events and always think of the ball as being in your court.

Step three: Make regular contact with support workers

When you work under pressure in an office environment, there are usually people around you who can sympathise or spread the load. Delegating even small parts of a task not only makes a physical impression on the work to be done, but also has a positive psychological effect and can therefore reduce the burden considerably. When you come under pressure in your home office, there's a distance barrier between you and your support system, and this is when feelings of isolation are most likely to kick in.

Regardless of the type of work that you do, there are usually some people that you rely on or work closely with.

✔ Be friendly with your team and colleagues in regular, positive but brief phone calls or e-mails. Ask light, open questions such as 'what's new?' that will prompt them to update you with all the gossip and changes afoot. Remember that you need to give something back, so encourage them to share their ups *and* downs with you and offer support and laughs in return.

Keeping in touch like this helps you in two ways: you learn what's going on in the office and you keep your office-based colleagues onside and friendly, which will be important when you need their help. If you've got into the habit of having these 'chats' and supporting others by phone, you will feel less alone when *you* are the one needing help or a friendly ear.

Step four: Join or start a local group for people in the same boat

This one isn't for everyone but a joining or setting up a group of like-minded home-workers or a professional group with interests in your field could be just the source of contacts you need to avoid isolation.

✔ Meet for breakfast, lunch, dinner, or drinks and get to know members personally as well as at a professional level. If you offer support to others they are likely to reciprocate when your spirits are in need of a lift. These environments will also help you to build your network and can be very constructive for your career.

TOP TIP

Don't put yourself under extra pressure by thinking you're the only home-worker who feels isolated. Compared with the busy office environment you're used to, you're bound to feel alone at times in your new work environment. It may help to know that there are many other home-workers just like you locally, thousands like you regionally and millions around the globe. The number is increasing rapidly. You can get in touch with

---

**them through the Internet, in chat rooms and
via professional bodies or trade-related sites.
If it gets too much, take your laptop out to
lunch or for a coffee! The change of scene
will do you good; just being in a restaurant
or café environment with people around
you making a bit of noise and bustle
can be enough to make the difference.**

Step six: Remember you're not super-human

Some people are very resourceful and self-reliant in their
working style, preferring to carry out their work alone and
solve their problems by themselves. If this sounds like you,
you may also recognise the tendency to shoulder all the
pressure and 'be strong'. Toughing out busy periods in this
way can put a lot of stress on your system, so confide in
people you trust and admit it if you need help – this isn't
a sign of weakness. No one can be strong all the time
and if you don't allow others to help you, you're adding
unnecessary pressure to your load.

TOP TIP
**Slot in a regular sanity check by setting aside
some time each week where you stop to
consider how you're feeling. Having some
time out to think about yourself, rather than
all your other tasks, will help you take**

**action to get the contact you need before
feelings of slight loneliness turn into
more serious isolation blues.**

Common mistakes

✗ You bombard your partner with questions

If you work at home and your partner or housemate
works in a busy environment, you may recognise this
scenario. You've spent the day closeted away, without
anyone to share your thoughts, and could really use a
good chat. But what if your partner is feeling drained by
the constant distractions or demands of others in his or
her work environment and just wants to be left alone?
Your needs at the end of the day are likely to be quite
different, so be sensitive and give some time and space
where it's required.

✗ You go too far the other way

Having encouraged visitors to drop by to stave off
isolation, you may find that once people know you're at
home they turn up too often and stay for too long. The
best solution, as you can imagine, is all about balance:
for productivity's sake you may need to set a few
parameters to manage this type of distraction without
discouraging it completely.

✗ You have too many 'virtual' contacts

The Internet can be great for making contact with others
in your field or other home-workers, but this level of
interaction will never replace real one-to-one human

communication. Even if you're pushed for time, it's well worth making the effort to talk to people face-to-face regularly.

STEPS TO SUCCESS

✔ Before you take the plunge of working from home full time, think about whether you're naturally suited to it or whether you're likely to find it lonely and tough. If you do go ahead, make some plans about how you'll get enough contact with other people to keep you happy.

✔ Make sure that you have the tools of your home-working trade set up from day one. The first few weeks can be very demanding after you change your work environment, and you may feel the need to prove yourself as a successful home-worker. You don't need to be coping with technology teething problems on top of all this pressure.

✔ Home-working doesn't necessarily mean that you never visit your colleagues or see the whites of your boss's eyes! You can still attend important meetings, training and social events.

✔ Make sure that you keep on top of changes back at the office by your informal contact with colleagues and support workers. The onus will be on you to make contact and ask questions. You don't need to be heavy-handed about this; a simple e-mail or phone call to say hello, and to ask how things are, is all you need.

✔ Make new contacts in your local area so that you don't rely too heavily on calls to your work colleagues for support. The advantages are that you will increase your network at the same time as getting the face-to-face contact you require.

✔ Create a backdrop of (appropriate!) noise if you find silence oppressive. Having music blaring out might not be the best idea (especially if you find yourself scrabbling to find the 'off' button on your stereo when your boss rings you unexpectedly), but low-key music or talk radio will help you feel as if you're not completely on your own.

✔ Don't let 'being strong' become your Achilles heel; you're only human and there's only so much you can take on and do well. Ask for help if you need it rather than struggling on.

Useful links

European Telework Online:

www.eto.org.uk

International Telework Association and Council:

www.telecommute.org